How to Be a
ROMAN SOLDIER

by Catherine M. Andronik

PEBBLE
a capstone imprint

Pebble is published by Capstone,
1710 Roe Crest Drive, North Mankato, Minnesota 56003
capstonepub.com

Copyright © 2026 by Capstone. All rights reserved. No part of this publication may be reproduced in whole or in part, or stored in a retrieval system, or transmitted in any form or by any means, electronic, mechanical, photocopying, recording, or otherwise, without written permission of the publisher.

Library of Congress Cataloging-in-Publication Data is available on the Library of Congress website.

ISBN: 9798875226830 (hardcover)
ISBN: 9798875234361 (paperback)
ISBN: 9798875234378 (ebook PDF)

Summary: Journey back in time to the Roman Empire and become a soldier! Learn about their training, tactics, weapons, and more. Then find out if you have what it takes to join the army and defend the empire.

Editorial Credits
Editor: Alison Deering; Designer: Bobbie Nuytten; Media Researcher: Svetlana Zhurkin; Production Specialist: Whitney Schaefer

Image Credits
Alamy: Lanmas, 13; Bridgeman: © Look and Learn, 7, Lebrecht History, 21; Getty Images: duncan1890, 15, 24; Shutterstock: adolf martinez soler (stone wall), cover and throughout, Alexandr Chernushkin, 16, Anwarul Kabir Photo, 10, Aron M, 9, Burak Erdal, cover (bottom left), Jennifer Nyman, cover (top), Lakeview Images, 22, Liliya Butenko, 14, Massimo Todaro, 17, 19, 25, 27, meunierd, 12, Mikko-Pekka Salo, 11, Monsalvettshop, 6, Sammy33, 23, Vuk Kostic, 5, 29, Yip Po Yu (texture), cover and throughout

Any additional websites and resources referenced in this book are not maintained, authorized, or sponsored by Capstone. All product and company names are trademarks™ or registered® trademarks of their respective holders.

Printed and bound in the USA. PO 006276

Table of Contents

Introduction
Welcome to Ancient Rome 4

Chapter 1
Are You Roman Soldier Material? 6

Chapter 2
Weaponry................................... 14

Chapter 3
Which Job Is for You?........................ 18

Chapter 4
A Soldier's Life 24

Roman Soldier Test............................... 30

Glossary... 31

Index 32

About the Author 32

Words in **bold** are in the glossary.

Introduction

Welcome to Ancient Rome

So, you want to be a Roman soldier? Get ready to journey back in time to Rome in the year 157.

The Roman Empire is huge and powerful. Everyone living in the empire follows Roman laws. Many speak Latin—the Roman language. They practice the Roman religion. Soldiers help defend the empire and extend its reach.

It is a great honor to become a Roman soldier. But the life of a soldier is also filled with danger.

Do YOU have what it takes to join the ranks of the Roman army?

Chapter 1

Are You Roman Soldier Material?

To be considered for the job of Roman soldier, you must be able to answer yes to ALL of the following questions:

1. Are you a Roman citizen?
2. Are you between the ages of 17 and 35?
3. Are you male?
4. Are you at least 5 feet 7 inches (170 centimeters) tall?
5. Do you have good eyesight and hearing?
6. Can you pass the physical exam?

Tip #1: Let's Get Physical!

The physical exam is difficult! It includes marching 20 miles (32 kilometers) in 5 hours, while wearing heavy armor.

Did you answer yes to all the questions? Congratulations! You can join the Roman army. You have four months of training ahead of you. You'll march long distances to improve your stamina. You'll do exercises to improve your strength. You'll practice fighting using a heavy wooden sword.

Being part of the army takes **discipline** and teamwork. You'll take orders from your commander. If you don't obey, you'll face physical punishment. You'll learn to work with your fellow soldiers.

Finally, your training is finished. If you were successful, it is time to take an oath. You will swear to protect Rome for the next 25 years! During the ceremony, you and a fellow soldier stand face to face. Your swords rest on the body of a pig.

You receive a piece of lead with your name and other identifying details inscribed on it. As long as you are a soldier of Rome, you will carry this in a little leather bag hung around your neck.

Tip #2: No Girls Allowed

Females are not allowed to join the Roman army. The only warrior women in ancient Rome are gladiators—people who fight for public entertainment.

A Roman soldier is always part of a larger group. The largest grouping in the army is the **legion**. There are between 4,000 and 6,000 men in a legion.

The group you'll get to know much better is your **century**. It has about 80 men. Your leader is a **centurion**.

It is time to say goodbye to your family and your old life. You may not see your family again until your 25 years of service in the Roman army are over.

Chapter 2
Weaponry

Now that you are a soldier, you will start using real weapons. You'll need two swords. The first is a **gladius**. It is about 2 feet (61 centimeters) long. This sword is used for battle in tight spaces.

Your other sword is longer. It is called a **spatha**. It is especially useful if you're fighting on horseback.

You'll also need a shield to protect your body. You and your fellow soldiers can use your shields to form a wall in a battle.

Tip #3: Were Gladiators Soldiers?

Entertainment in ancient Rome included fights among gladiators. Fighters used weapons—including the gladius!—to show off their skills. A few retired soldiers volunteered to become gladiators. But most gladiators were enslaved people.

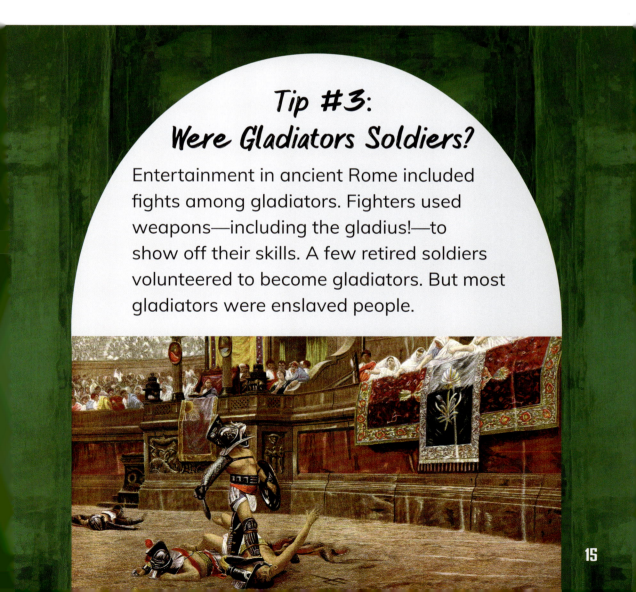

Your swords and shields are too heavy to carry with you everywhere. In case of sudden danger, you will want a short dagger. To complete your collection, you'll buy a **javelin** as well as a bow and arrows.

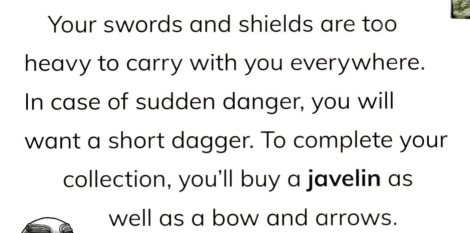

You'll also need body armor to cover your torso. One type is made of iron and bronze strips linked together. To protect your head, you will need a good helmet made of iron and leather.

But be prepared. Your armor is heavy! It weighs about 45 to 55 pounds (20 to 25 kilograms), not including your weapons! You will carry it wherever you march.

Chapter 3

Which Job Is for You?

Most soldiers in the Roman army are foot soldiers. You could also ask about joining the cavalry. In this role, you would ride horses into battle. Horses and horse armor are expensive, so it helps to be from a noble family.

Are you clever and good with your hands? The army may have a job for you as an engineer, **architect**, or other specialist. You might be put in charge of soldiers constructing a fort or building a bridge.

You might also be asked to design, create, and maintain weapons used at a distance. The scorpion is a small **catapult** that can be operated by a single soldier. It has a longer range than an arrow shot from a bow.

The **ballista** is larger and more powerful. It can fire a heavy boulder or a long spike. It is capable of hitting targets at a distance of 1,500 feet (457 meters).

There is also the **onager**. This wheeled weapon can fire 150 pounds (68 kg) of stones at a wall and break through it.

If you want to be promoted to an even higher role, you'll need to know how to read, write, and do basic math. Not everyone in Rome has this kind of education.

If you're especially good with numbers, you might become a **standard bearer**. In this job, you'll keep track of your unit's money. You will be paid very well.

Tip #4:
Animals on the Battlefield

Growing up in Rome, you may have seen horse-drawn chariots in shows at the local coliseum. But the Roman army hasn't used that style of fighting for centuries. They do very occasionally use elephants—something they learned fighting against North Africans.

Chapter 4

A Soldier's Life

Some Roman soldiers survive many battles in a lifetime. Some never see combat. But all of them spend a lot of time marching from place to place. Along the way, you must build camp.

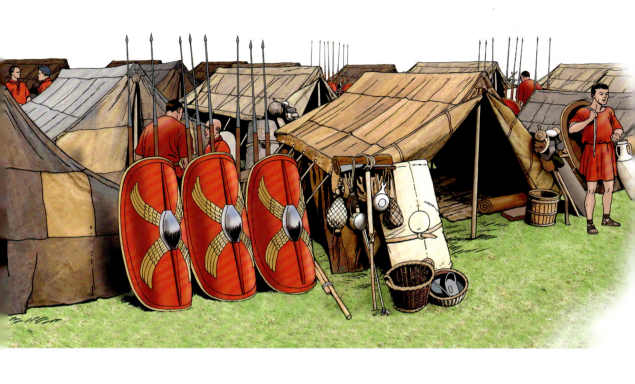

To do so, you help dig a ditch and set up a wall of spikes around it. You sleep eight men to a tent. You must cook your own dinner. You grind and boil wheat into a hot cereal or bake it into bread.

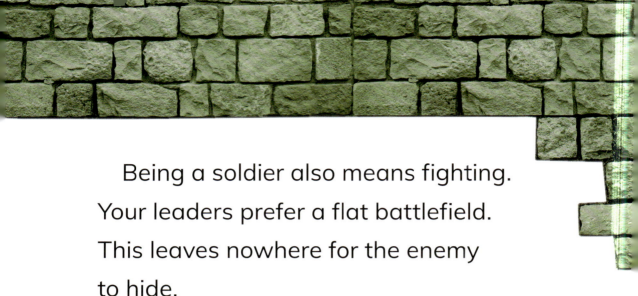

Being a soldier also means fighting. Your leaders prefer a flat battlefield. This leaves nowhere for the enemy to hide.

When battle comes, you put on your armor. The army divides into lines and groups. Some soldiers cluster together. They hold their shields together in front of them, forming a wall.

Soldiers on the front lines begin firing arrows and javelins. Then it's time—behind the shield wall, you and your fellow Roman soldiers begin to move forward.

When you get close to the enemy, you draw your swords and charge. Who will be victorious?

The life of a soldier is difficult, dirty, and dangerous. For 25 years, you live according to the orders of your commanders. But you can also be proud. You represent the Roman Empire.

Only 50 percent of soldiers survive their time in the Roman army. If you are one of them, you will receive a generous reward—10 years' pay!

Finally, you can see your family again. You'll spend the rest of your life telling them stories of everything you've seen and done as a Roman soldier.

Roman Soldier Test

1. Which is NOT required to become a Roman soldier?
- a. be at least 5 feet 7 inches (170 cm) tall
- b. know how to ride a horse
- c. have good eyesight

2. What is a Roman soldier's sword called?
- a. a gladius
- b. a dagger
- c. a javelin

3. How many years does a Roman soldier serve?
- a. one year
- b. 10 years
- c. 25 years

4. The most powerful catapult is called:
- a. a ballista
- b. a gladius
- c. an onager

5. In battle, Roman soldiers form a wall behind their:
- a. elephants
- b. horses
- c. shields

Answers: 1) b, 2) a, 3) c, 4) c, 5) a

If you got all the answers correct, you're ready to become a Roman soldier! If you missed a few, try again.

Glossary

architect (AR-kuh-tekt)—a person who designs buildings

ballista (buh-LIS-tuh)—a catapult

catapult (KAT-uh-puhlt)—a weapon used to hurl rocks, liquid, or other items at an enemy

centurion (sen-TOOR-ee-uhn)—the commander of a century in the Roman army

century (SEN-chuh-ree)—a grouping of about 80 men in the Roman army

discipline (DIS-uh-plin)—self-control and the ability to follow the rules

gladius (GLEY-dee-uhs)—a sword about two feet long

javelin (JAV-uh-lin)—a long spear

legion (LEE-juhn)—a grouping of about 5,000 men in the Roman army

onager (ON-uh-jer)—a large, powerful catapult

spatha (SPAH-thuh)—a sword about three feet long

standard bearer (STAN-derd BAIR-er)—the person who kept track of the money in an army unit

Index

armor, 7, 16–17, 18, 26

battles, 24, 26, 27

centuries, 12
centurions, 12
ceremonies, 10
coliseums, 23

education, 22

gladiators, 11, 15

horses, 14, 18, 23

jobs, 18, 20, 22

legions, 12
lifestyle, 24, 25, 28

physical exam, 6, 7

requirements, 6
Roman Empire, 4, 28

training, 8, 10

weapons, 10, 14–15, 16–17, 20, 26–27

years of service, 10, 13, 28

About the Author

Catherine M. Andronik is a high school teacher librarian who specializes in writing children's and young adult biographies. She shares her Connecticut home with a variety of rescue parrots and also enjoys showing her horse in western dressage.